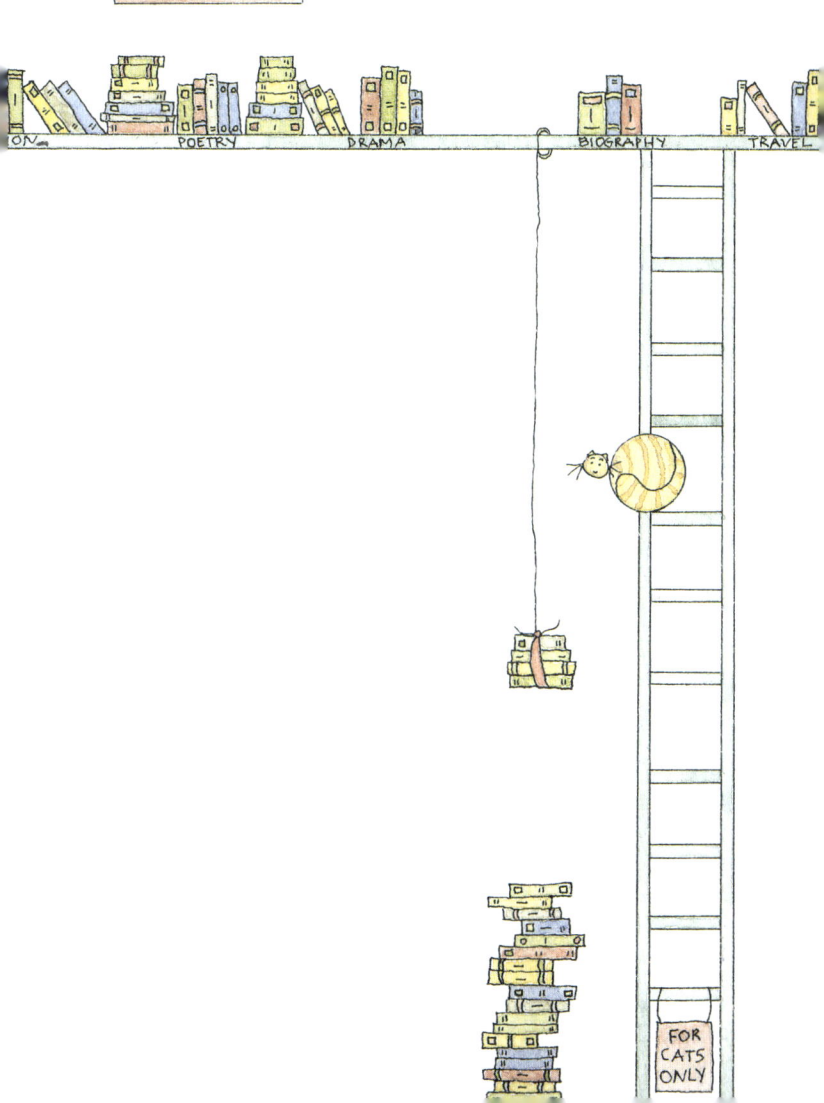

BOOKS ON MICE

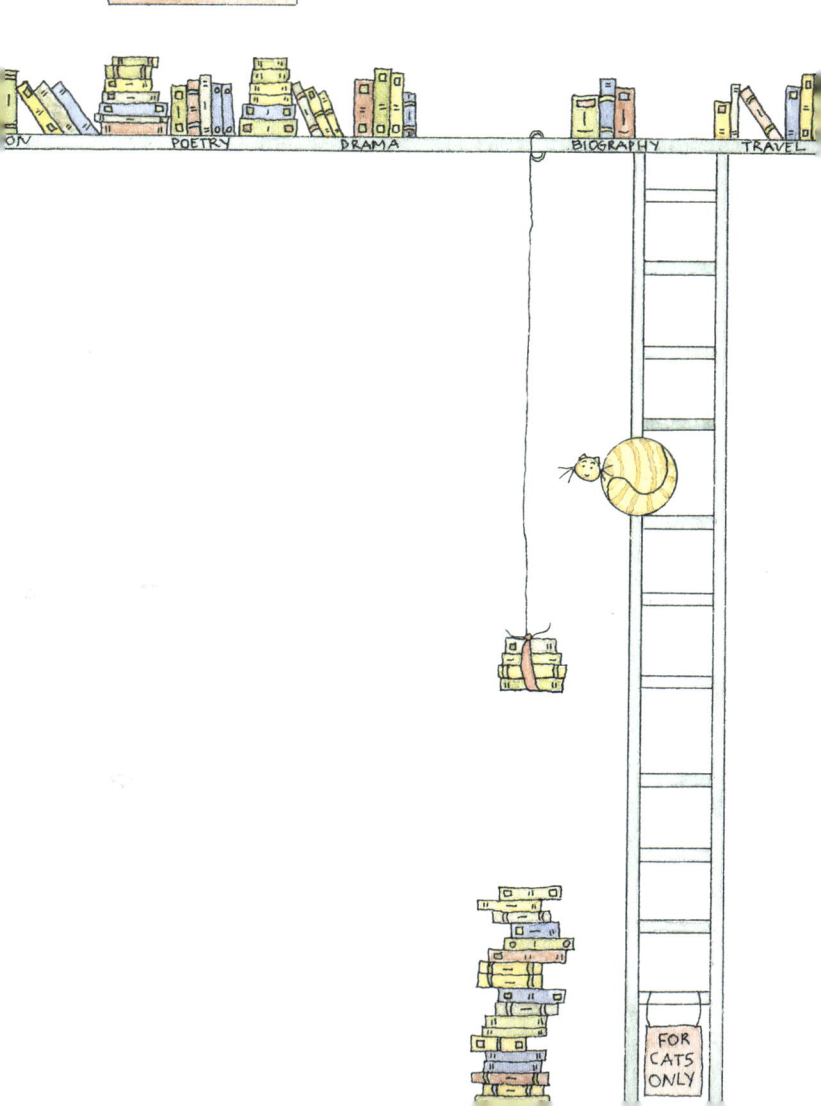

BOOKS ON MICE

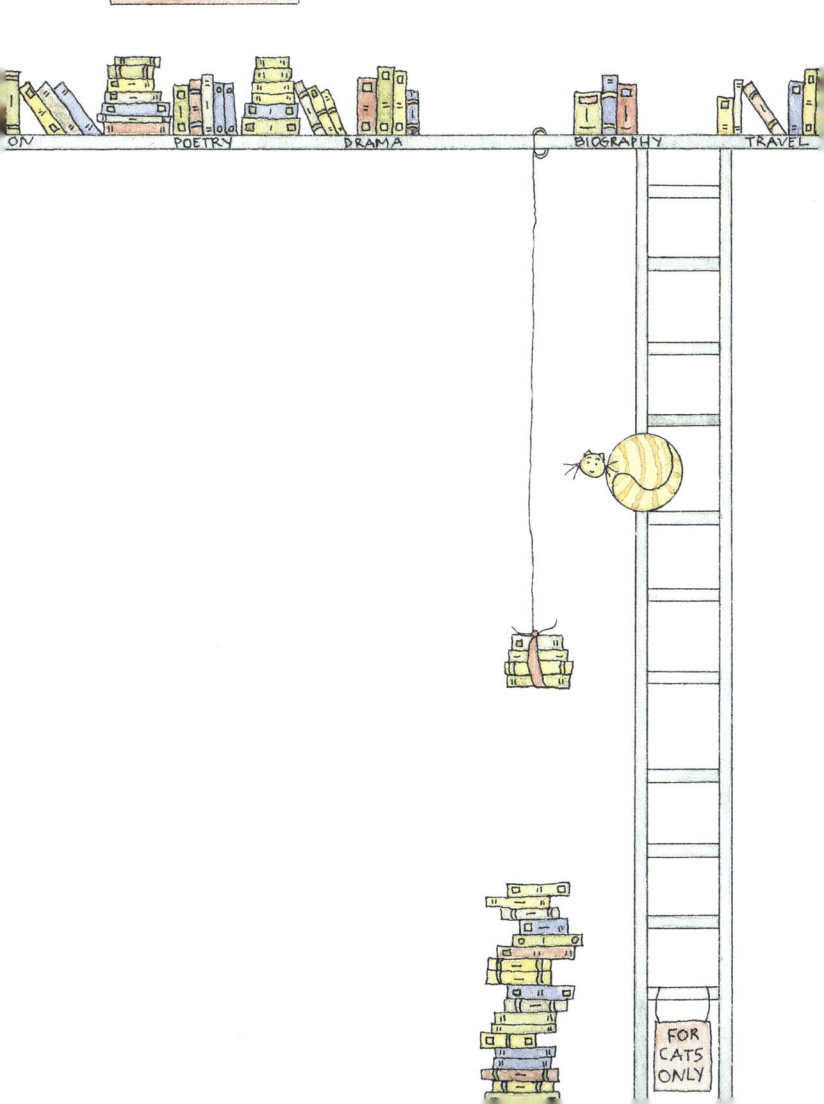

BOOKS ON MICE

FICTION POETRY DRAMA BIOGRAPHY TRAVEL

FOR CATS ONLY

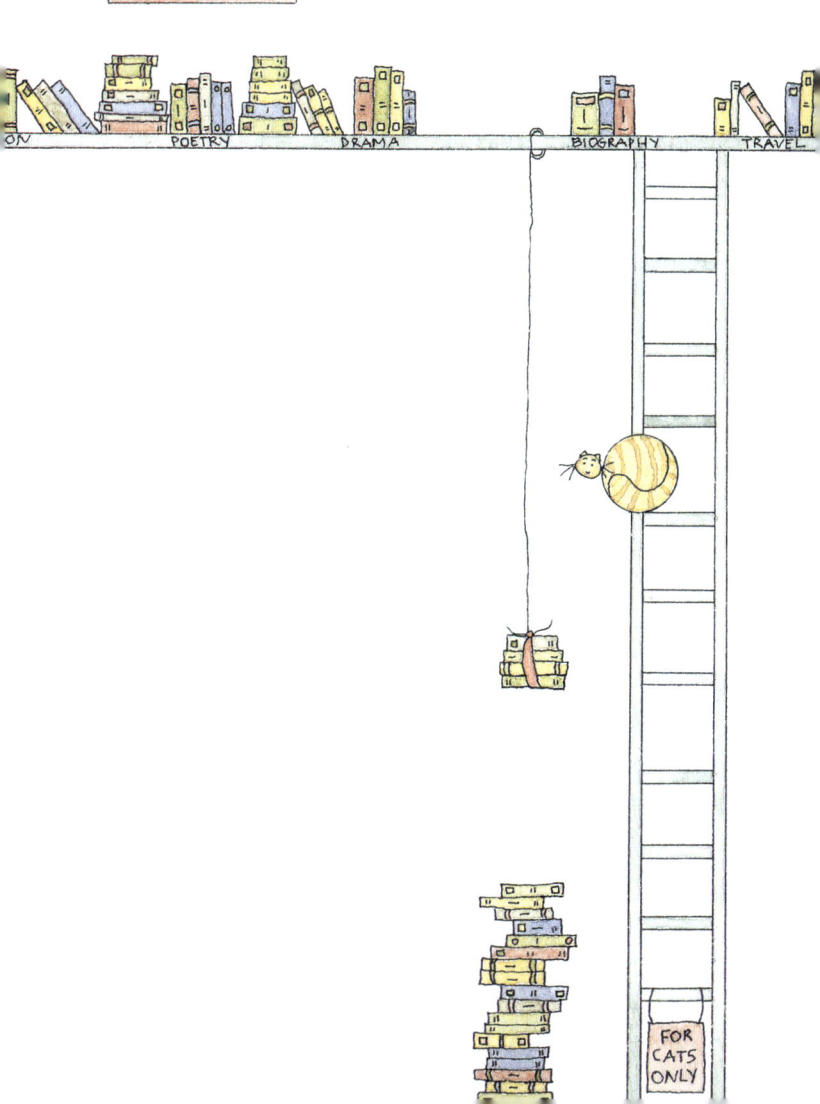

BOOKS ON MICE

ON POETRY DRAMA BIOGRAPHY TRAVEL

FOR CATS ONLY

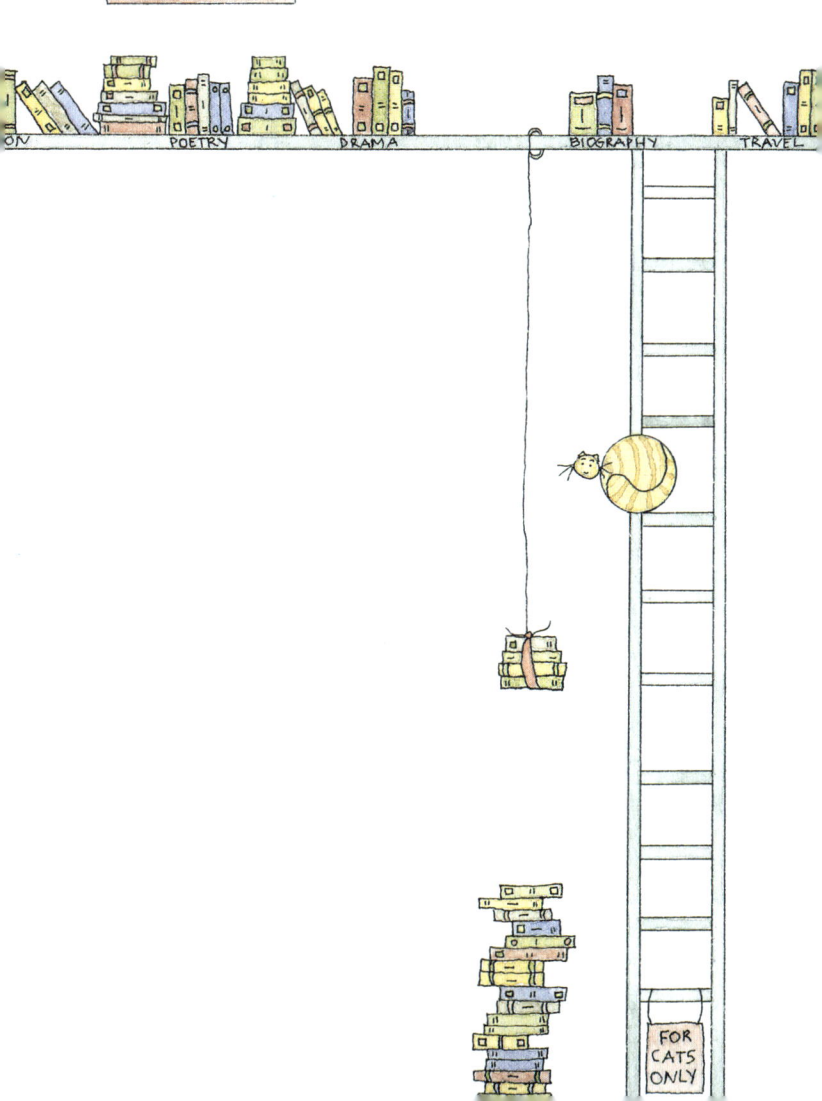

BOOKS ON MICE

POETRY   DRAMA   BIOGRAPHY   TRAVEL

FOR CATS ONLY

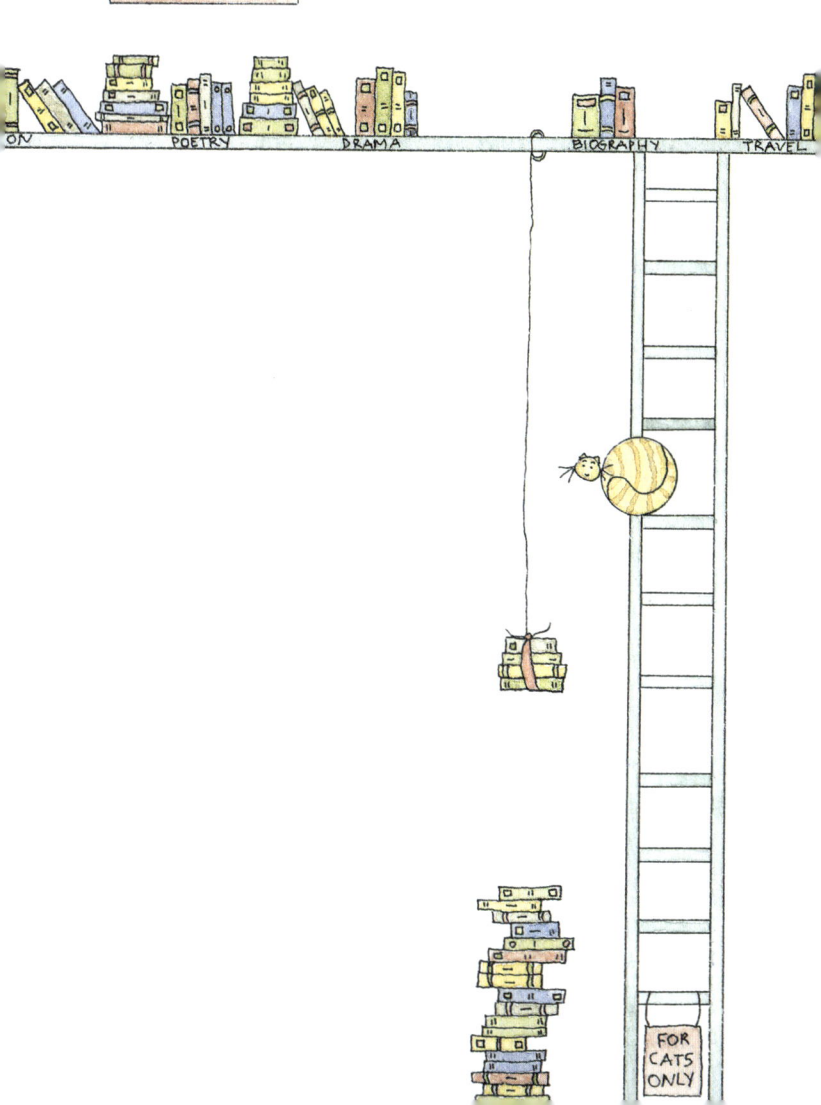

BOOKS ON MICE

POETRY   DRAMA   BIOGRAPHY   TRAVEL

FOR CATS ONLY

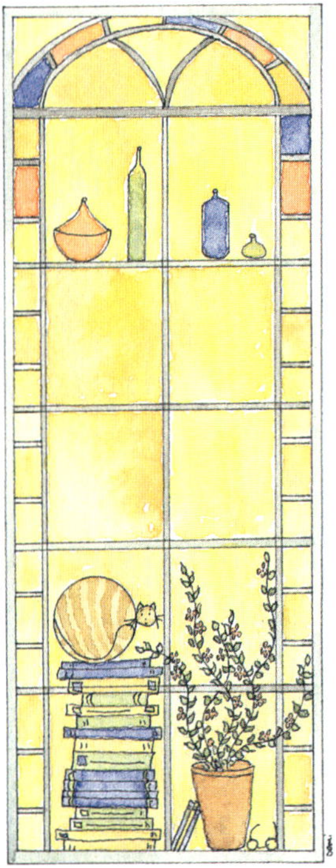

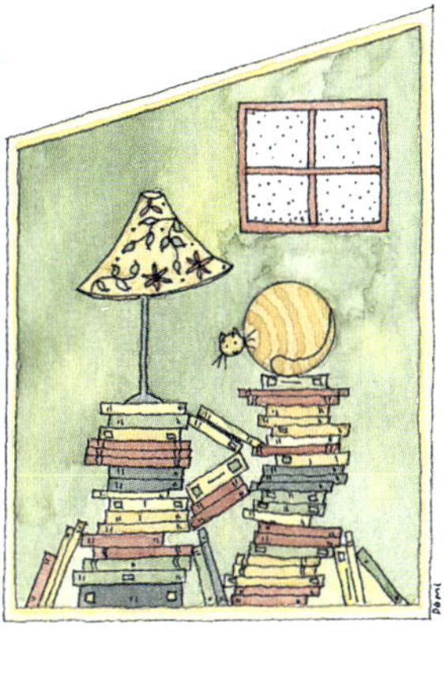

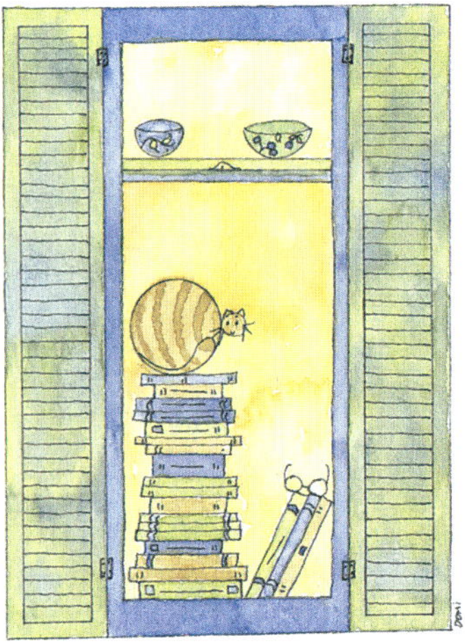

BOOKS ON MICE

FICTION POETRY DRAMA BIOGRAPHY TRAVEL

FOR CATS ONLY

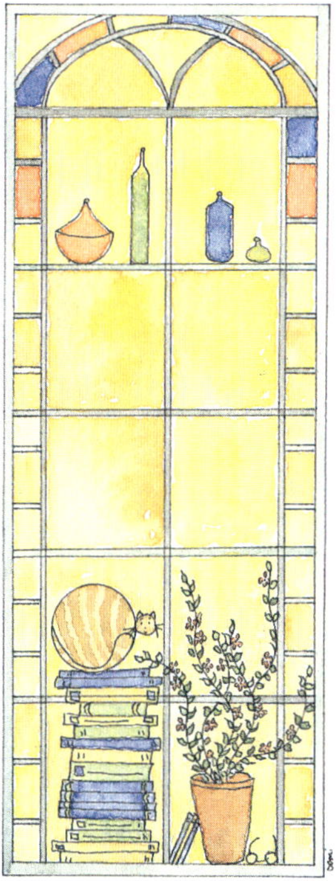

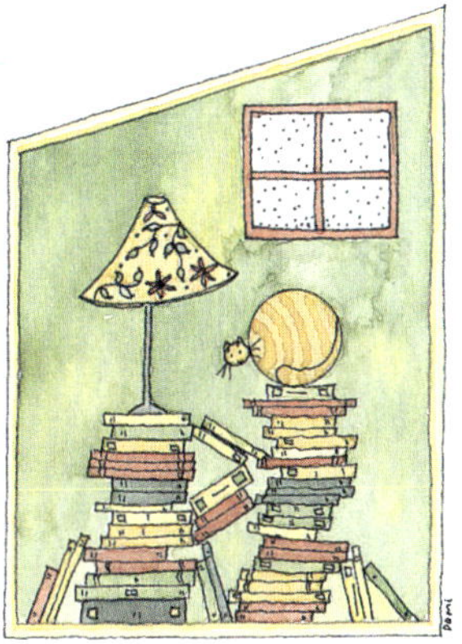

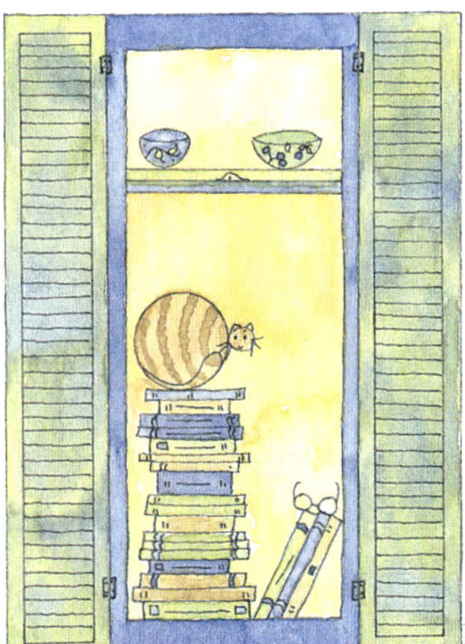

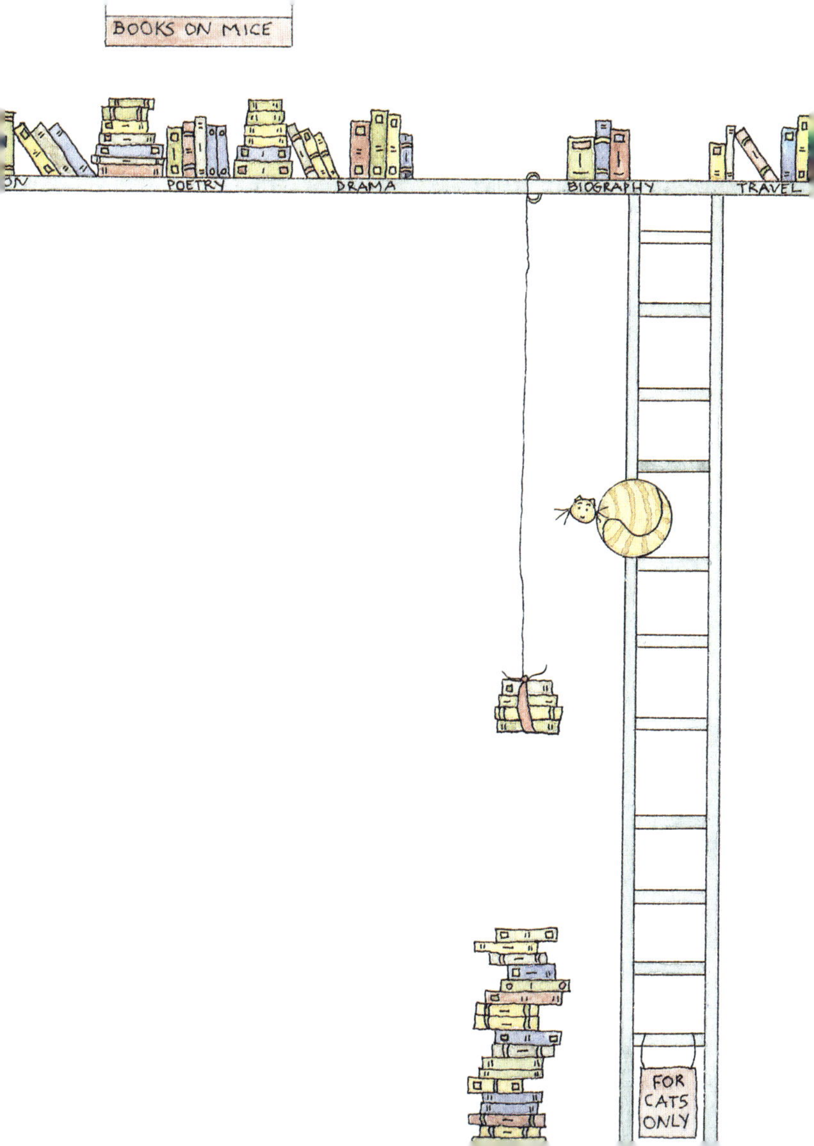

BOOKS ON MICE
ON
POETRY
DRAMA
BIOGRAPHY
TRAVEL
FOR CATS ONLY

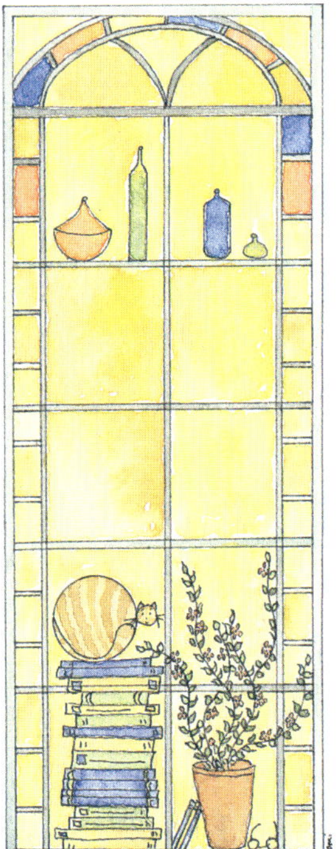

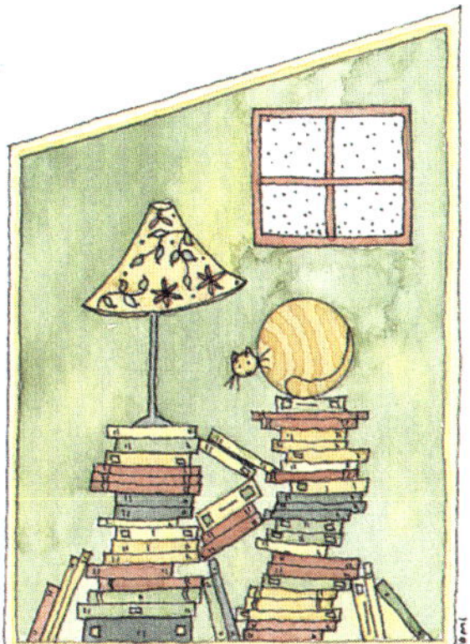

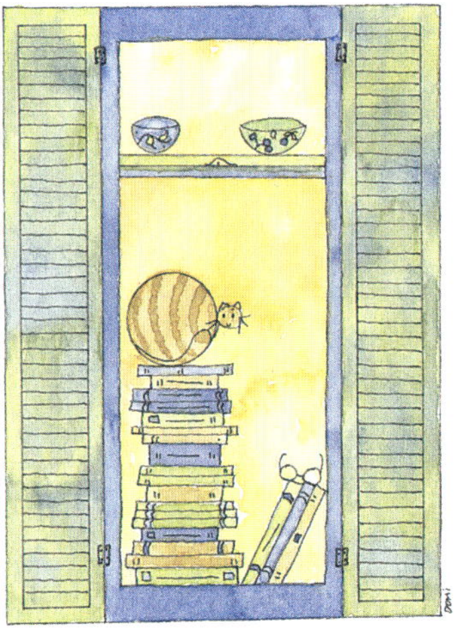

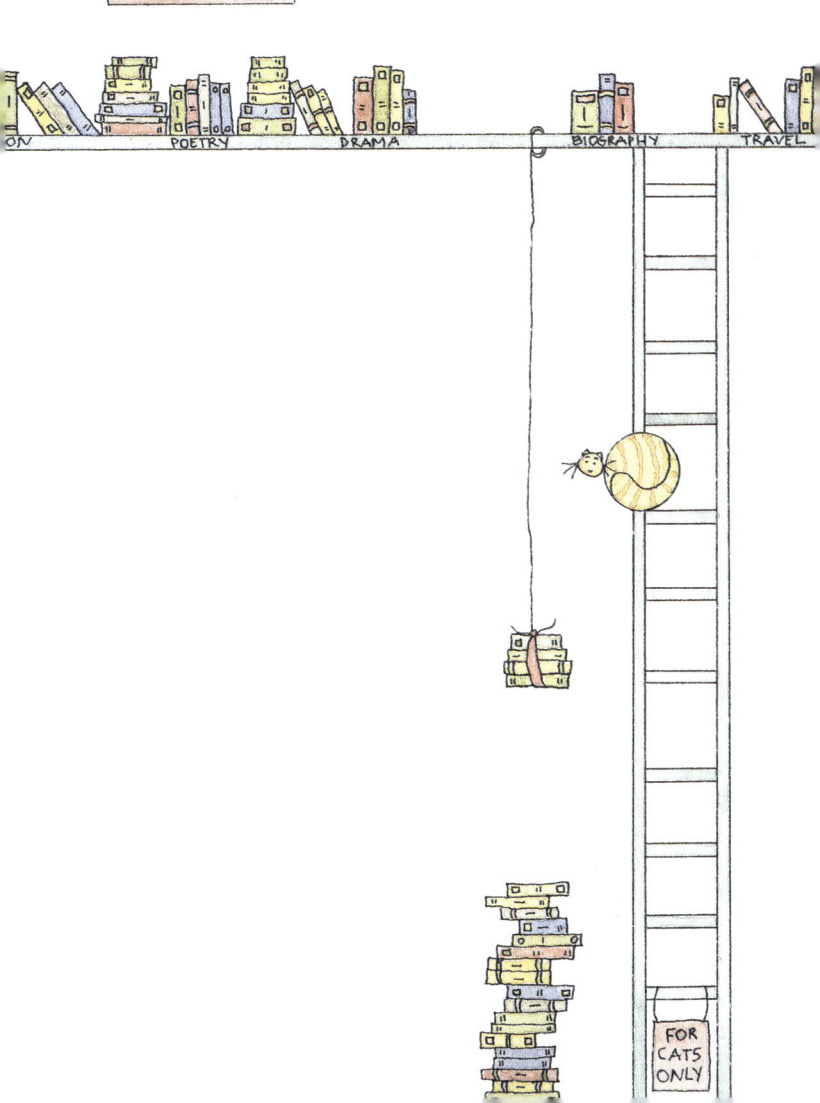

BOOKS ON MICE

FICTION · POETRY · DRAMA · BIOGRAPHY · TRAVEL

FOR CATS ONLY

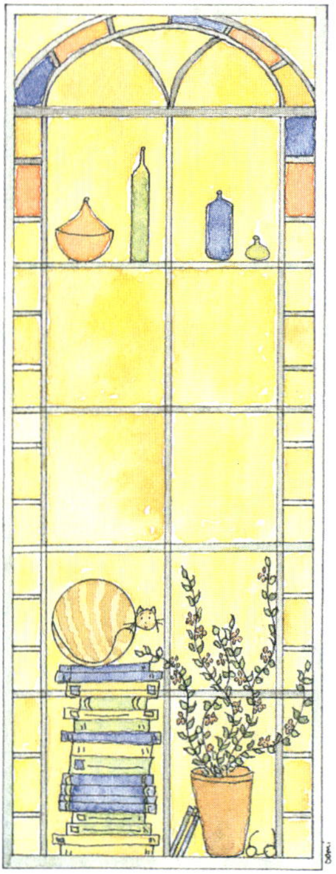

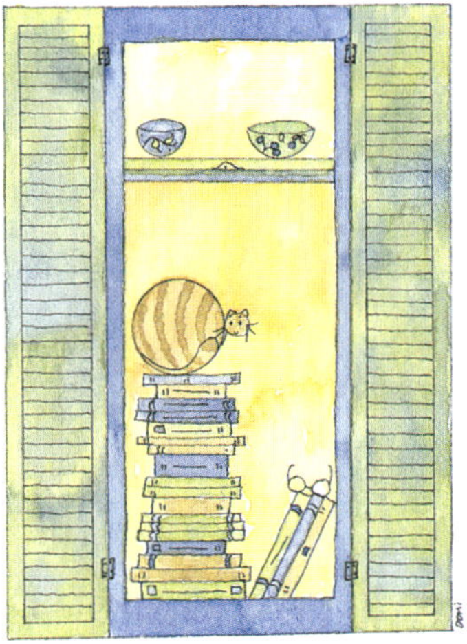

BOOKS ON MICE

POETRY   DRAMA   BIOGRAPHY   TRAVEL

FOR CATS ONLY

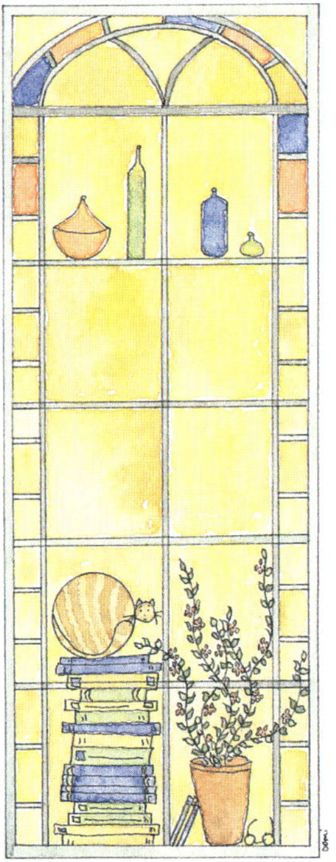

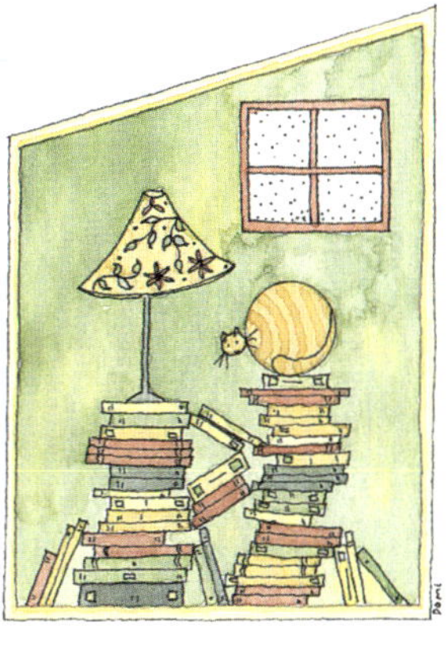

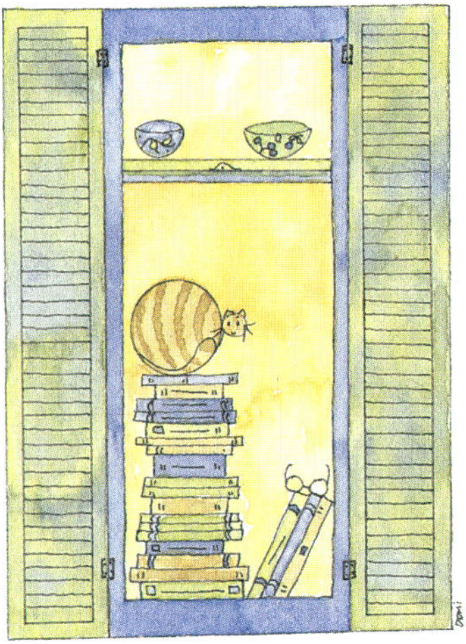

BOOKS ON MICE

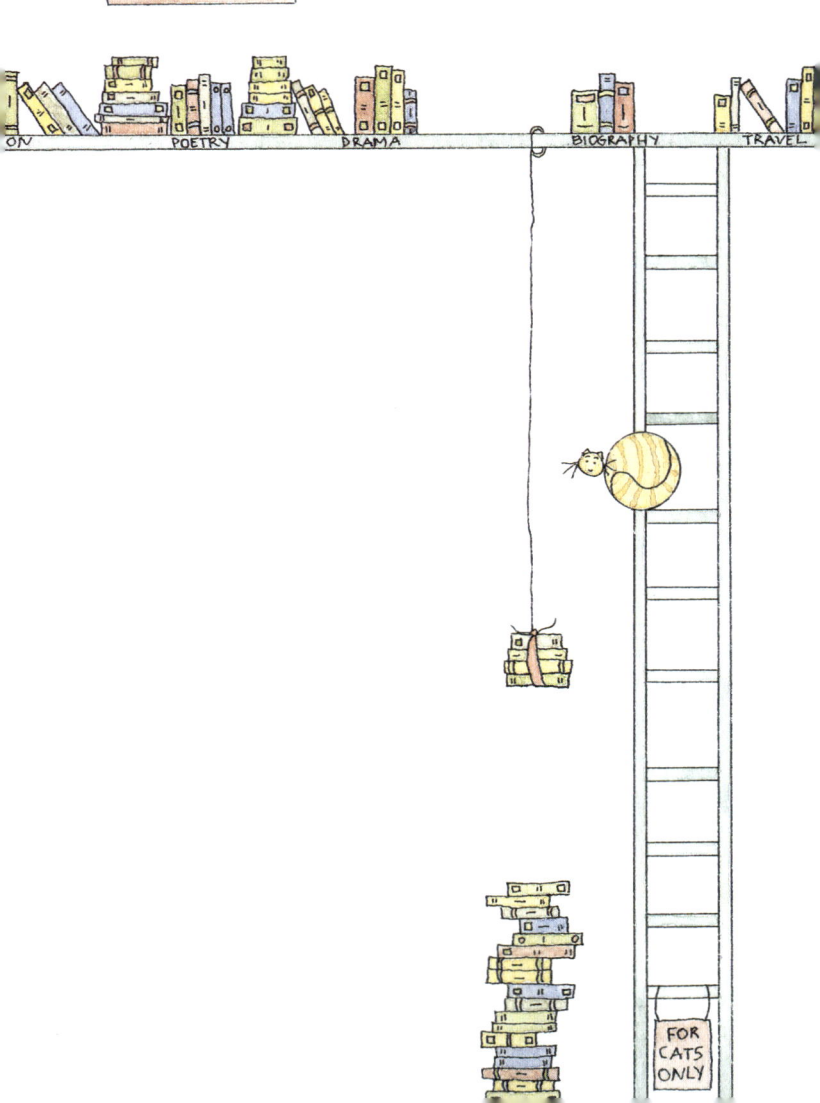

ON   POETRY   DRAMA   BIOGRAPHY   TRAVEL

FOR CATS ONLY

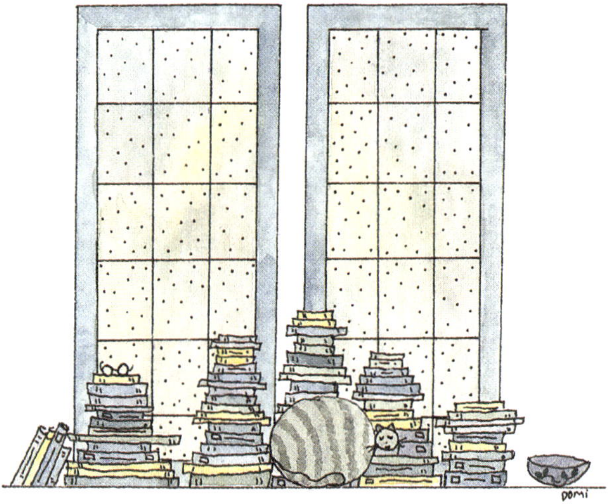
DOMI

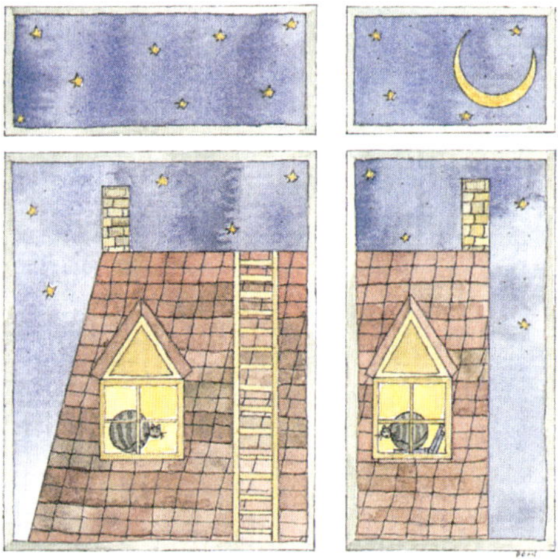

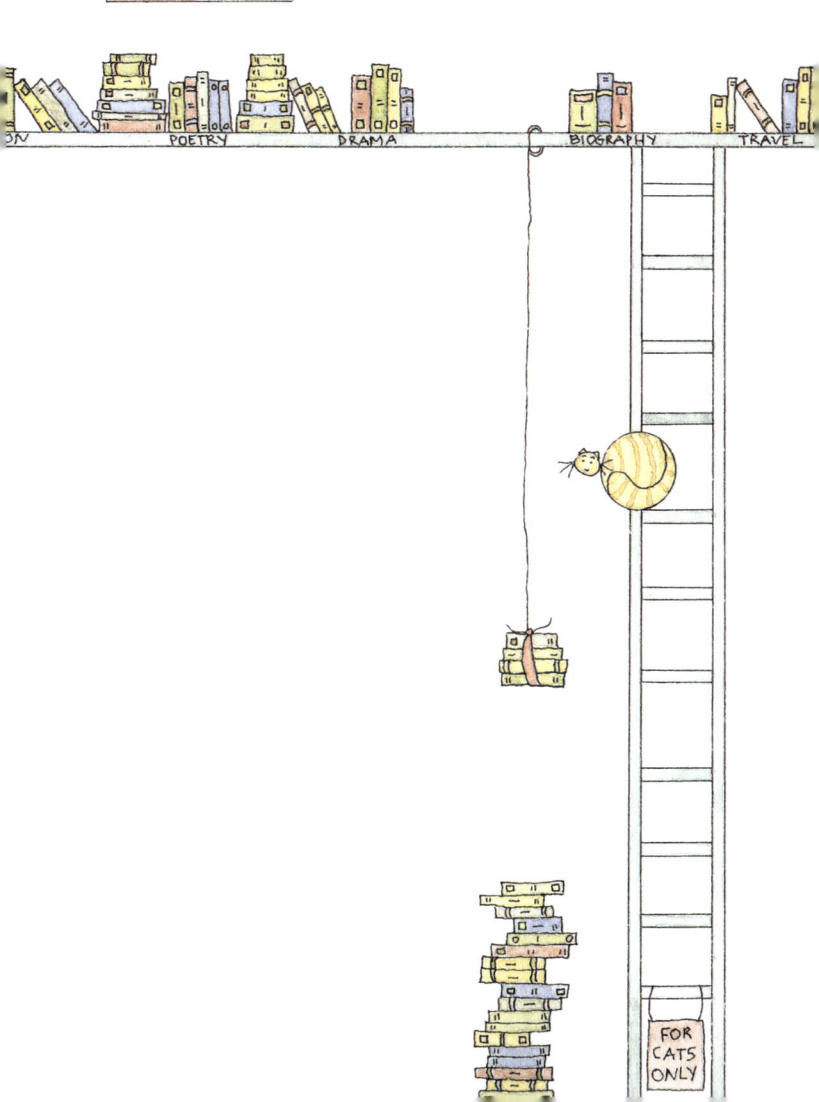

BOOKS ON MICE

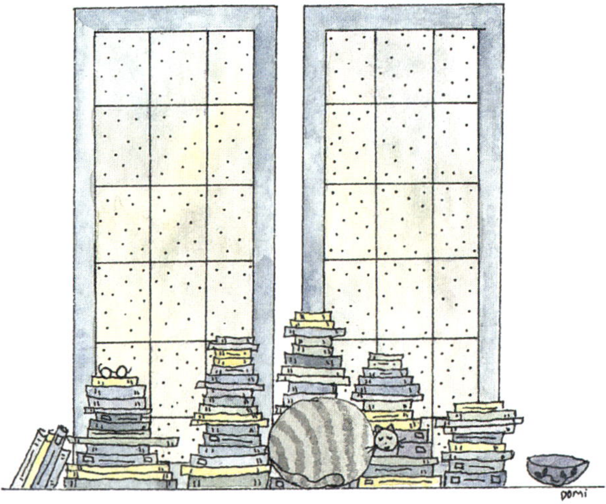
DOMI

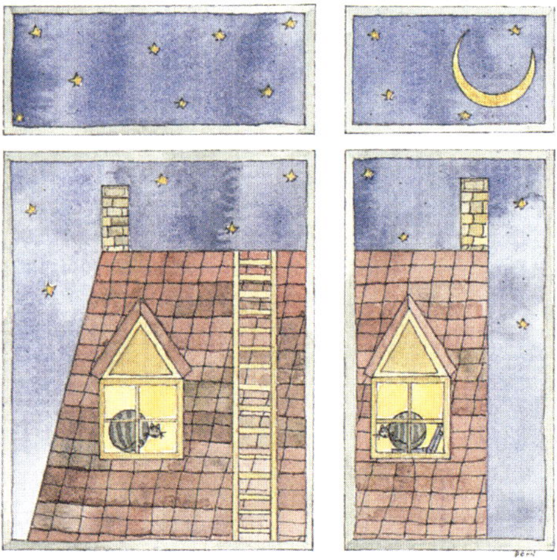

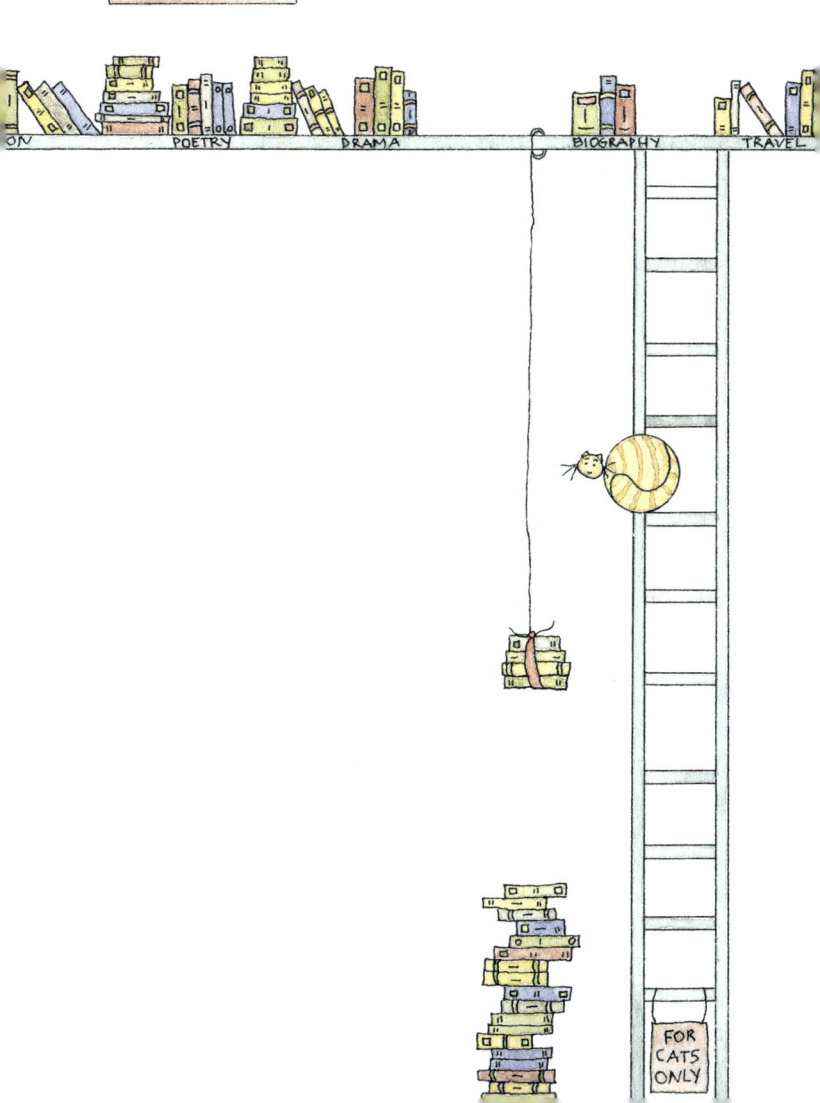

BOOKS ON MICE

ON · POETRY · DRAMA · BIOGRAPHY · TRAVEL

FOR CATS ONLY

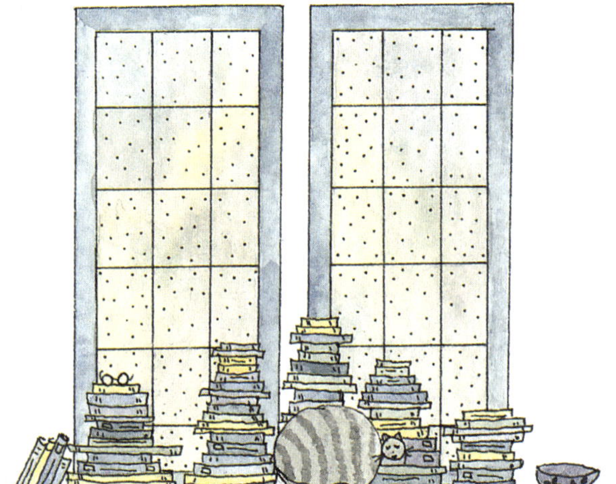
DOMI

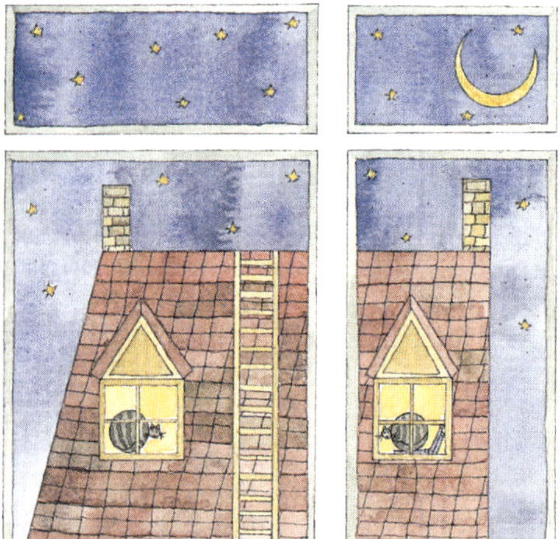

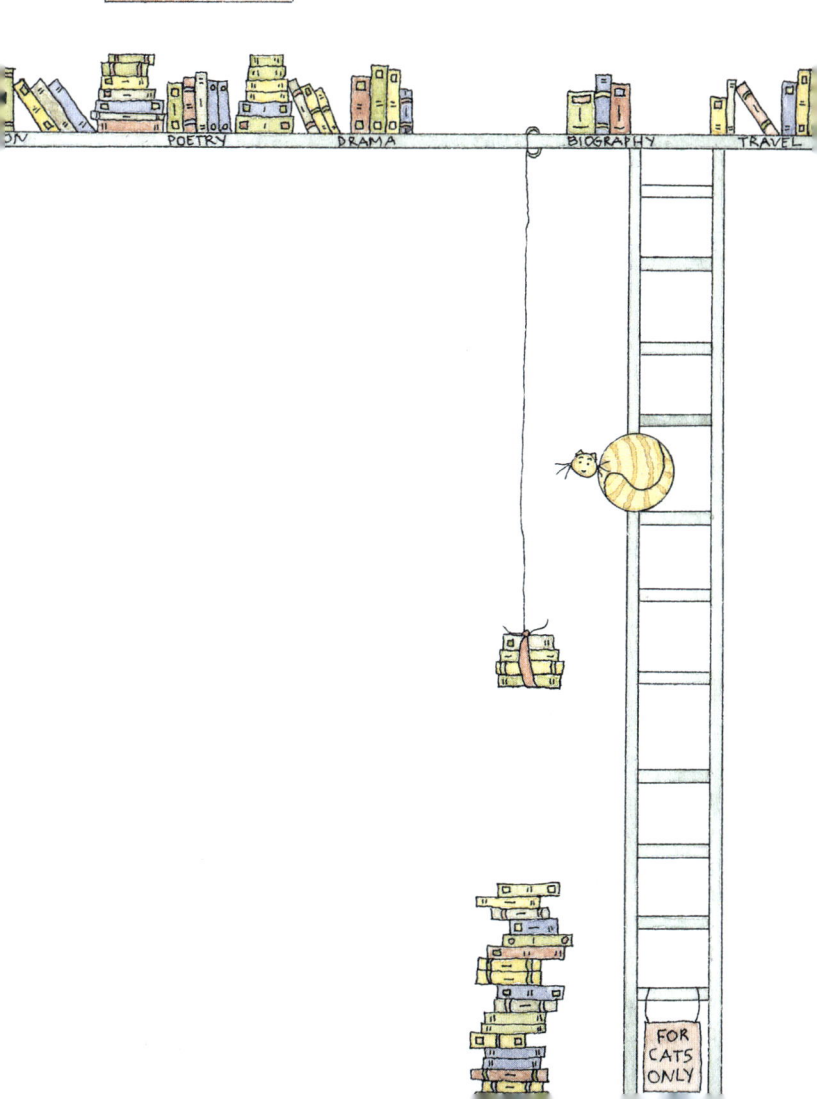

BOOKS ON MICE

POETRY　　DRAMA　　BIOGRAPHY　　TRAVEL

FOR CATS ONLY

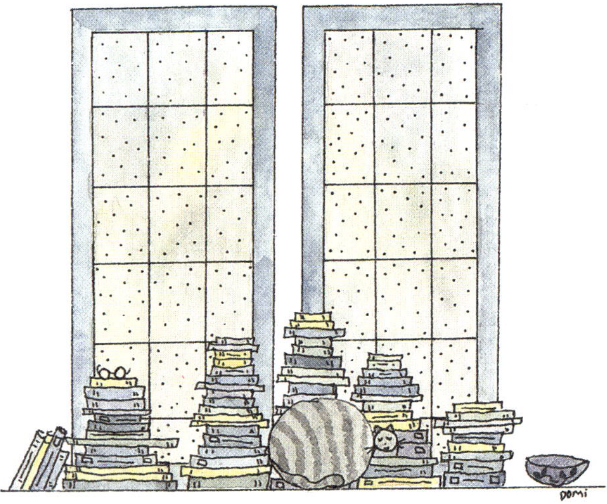
DOMI

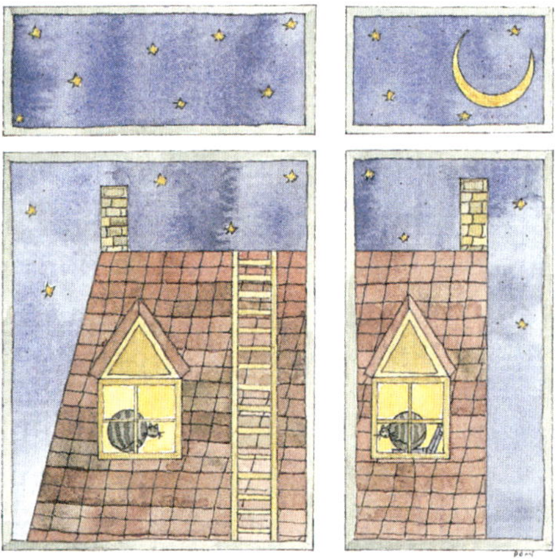

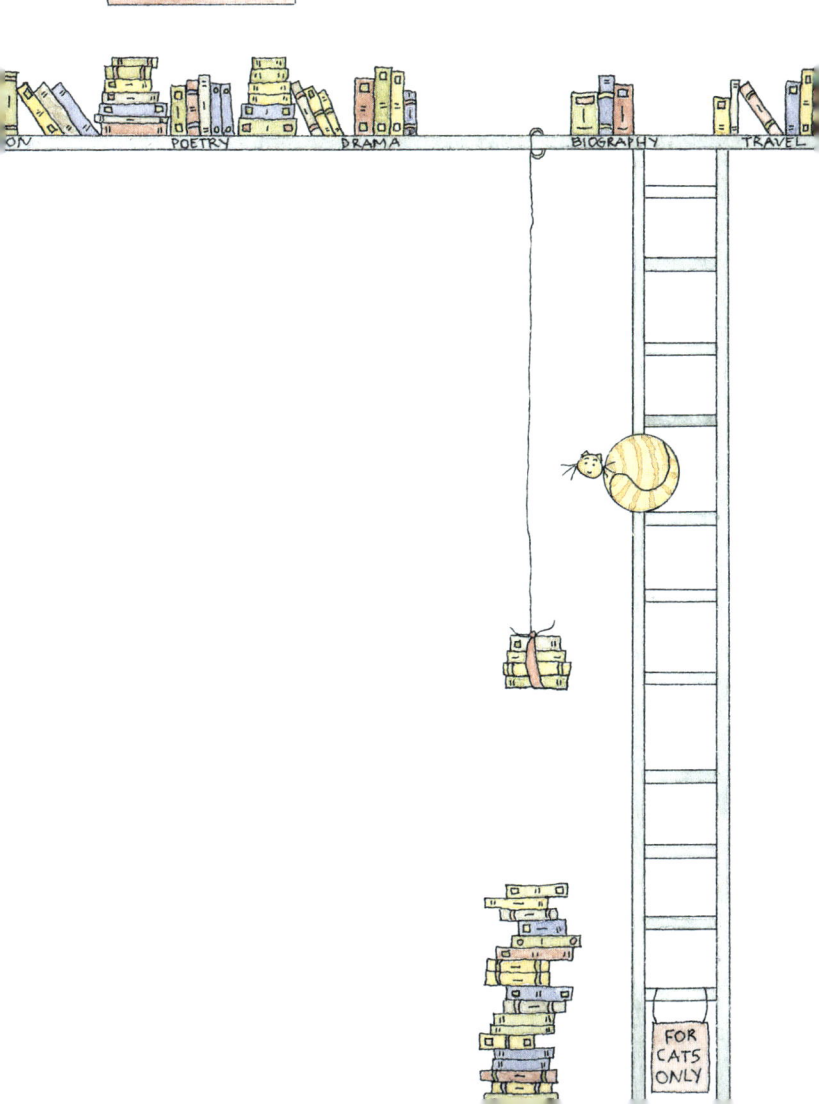

BOOKS ON MICE

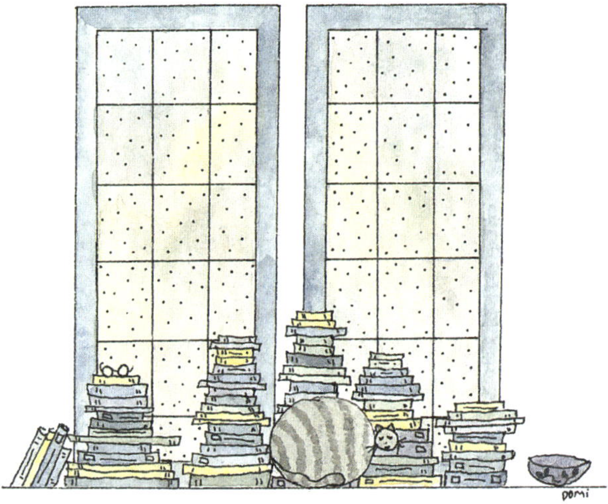
DOMI

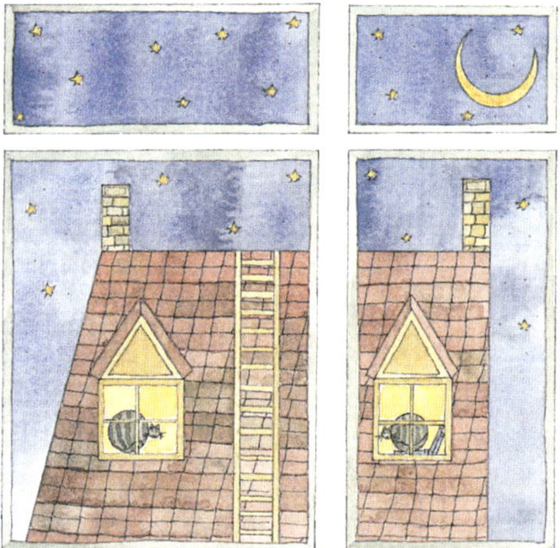

BOOKS ON MICE

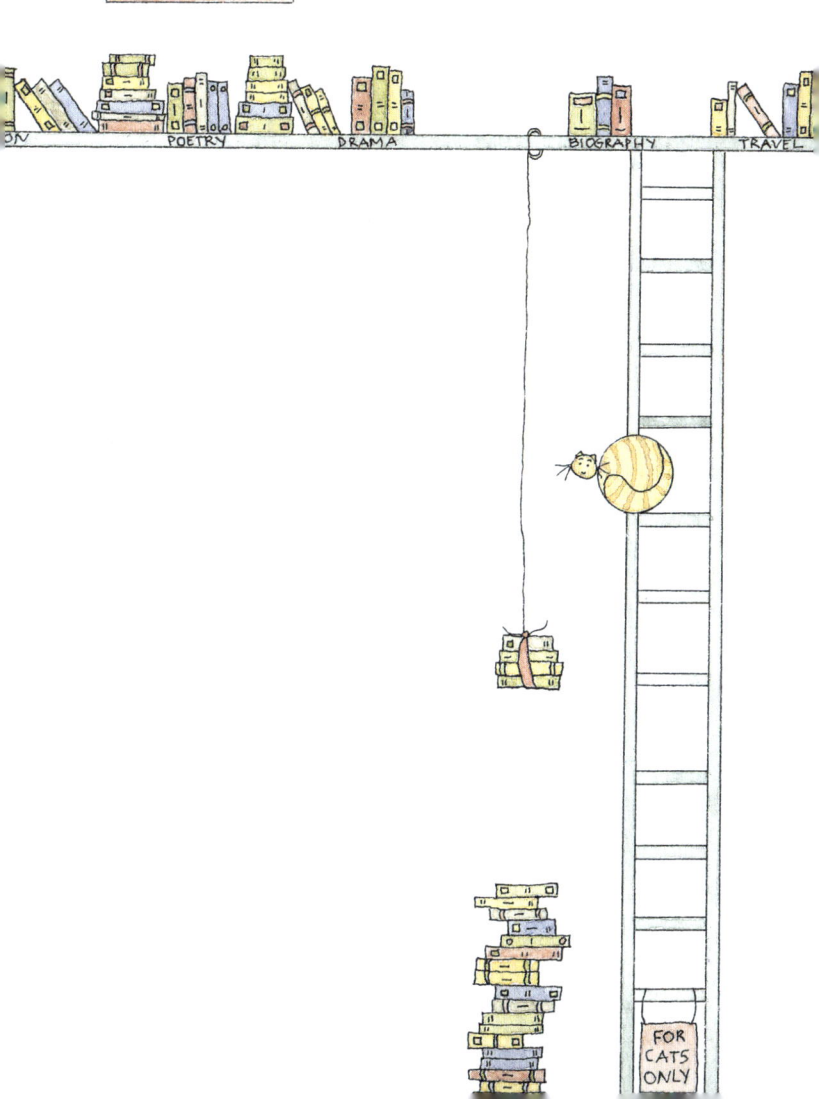

POETRY   DRAMA   BIOGRAPHY   TRAVEL

FOR CATS ONLY